S0-ANQ-004

Our Year with God

Our Year with God

A Child's Introduction to Catholic Holy Days and the Liturgical Year

Written by Natalie Kadela

Pauline
BOOKS & MEDIA
Boston

Nihil Obstat:
Rev. Alfred McBride, O.Praem.

Imprimatur:
† Bernard Cardinal Law
November 3, 1999

English translation of the *Doxology* by the International Consultation on English Texts.

Permission is granted to reproduce, duplicate, or photocopy the coloring pages included in this book.

The author extends special thanks to Virginia Helen Richards, FSP and Deborah Thomas Halpin, FSP for suggesting some of the activities included in this book.

Illustrations: Virginia Helen Richards, FSP (coloring pages), Helen Rita Lane, FSP

Copyright © 2000, Daughters of St. Paul

Printed and published in the U.S.A. by Pauline Books & Media, 50 Saint Pauls Avenue, Boston, MA 02130-3491.

www.pauline.org

Pauline Books & Media is the publishing house of the Daughters of St. Paul, an international congregation of women religious serving the Church with the communications media.

1 2 3 4 5 6   05 04 03 02 01 00

A Note to Parents and Teachers

The text, prayers and activities of *Our Year with God* are flexible enough to be adapted to the age of the children and to the settings in which they are being used. You are warmly encouraged to customize these materials to fit your own specific needs.

The activities are designed to give free reign to your children's creativity. The more they explore the motivations behind our liturgical seasons and holy days in order to express these through their projects, the more deeply will they assimilate the meanings of these important Church celebrations.

Enjoy helping your children discover the riches of the liturgical year, and have a holy year with God!

Contents

Our Year with God

We celebrate many special days during the year. We celebrate them with our families and friends. We celebrate birthdays, anniversaries, Mother's Day and Father's Day. We celebrate them with parties, or with customs that are the same year after year.

We give each year that we spend worshiping and loving God together a special name. Our year with God is called a *liturgical year.* Our Catholic Church also celebrates special days and seasons during the liturgical year. We honor Jesus, Mary and the saints at these times. We remember important events in their lives. We do this by going to church and by taking part in different activities and customs.

This book will teach you about some of the important seasons and days in our year with God. You will find a story about each special day of the liturgical year. You'll also find a prayer to say and some projects to do. At the back of the book, you'll even find pages to color for each special day!

We call some of the Church's special days *feast days.* We call others *holy days of obligation.* A holy day of obligation is a feast day that all Catholics are called to celebrate by taking part in the Eucharist (going to Mass). Joining together at Mass, we praise, adore and thank God for all the wonderful things he does for us.

Every Sunday of the year is a holy day of obligation. On Sundays we remember in a special way the *resurrection,* Jesus' rising from the dead. We celebrate by going to Mass on Sunday or on Saturday night. Our Church has other holy days of obligation, too. They are celebrated according to the needs of the people and the decisions of the bishops in each country. (**Note to parents and teachers:** For a listing of the holy days of obligation, please see page 92.)

When we understand our Church's special days and seasons, they help us to live more and more like Jesus. Our holy days and seasons help us grow closer to God and to one another.

Advent

dvent is a season of waiting. In Advent we wait for the most wonderful birthday of all—the birthday of Jesus! We also remember that Jesus will come again at the end of time. The Advent season of waiting lasts four weeks.

One of the things we do while we wait is get ready. If we are waiting for the birth of a new baby, we help our parents fix a room and get everything the baby will need. If we are waiting for a birthday, we plan ways to make it special for the birthday person.

In Advent, we remember the story of Mary, Jesus' mother, and Joseph, Jesus' foster father. We remember how they got ready for the coming of their baby. Mary and Joseph prepared a bed and clothing for Jesus. They prepared their hearts for Jesus with love and prayer.

Like Mary and Joseph, we must get ready to celebrate the birthday of Jesus on Christmas. We too must make room for Jesus in our churches, in our homes and especially in our hearts.

Our churches get ready for Christmas by putting out an *Advent wreath* for everyone to see. The circle of the wreath reminds us that God never had a beginning and will never have an end. The evergreen branches or leaves mean something, too. They stand for our hope that one day we will live with God forever. The flames of the four candles remind us that Jesus is the light of the world. They are also like the light of Jesus showing us the way to live. As we light a new candle each week, we see that the celebration of Jesus' birth is getting closer.

Three candles of the Advent wreath are purple. One candle is pink. Purple is the color of Advent. This color reminds us that we sin and need Jesus our Savior. In the liturgical year, the color purple stands for *penance*. Penance is something we freely choose to do to show that we are sorry for our sins. The purple candles of the Advent wreath remind us to make some little *sacrifices* to prepare for Christmas. (A sacrifice is doing something we don't especially like, or giving up something we do like.) We light the pink candle of the wreath on the Third Sunday of Advent. It stands for our joy that Christmas is almost here.

Our church and our priest also dress in the Advent color during this season of waiting. The *chasuble,* or sleeveless outer robe the priest wears at Mass, is purple. The cloth covering the altar may be purple, too.

We also get our homes ready for Jesus' birthday. We may have an Advent wreath on our table. We may hang up an *Advent calendar* to help count down the days until December 25. An Advent calendar has many little "doors." There is usually one to open for each day of December. Behind each door is a picture or a Bible quote that helps us to get ready for the birth of Jesus. We may also set up a crèche or nativity scene with a little stable and statues of Baby Jesus, Mary and Joseph, the shepherds and animals and the wise men. All these signs remind us of Jesus' upcoming birthday and the true meaning of Christmas.

But the most important thing we do in Advent is to get our hearts ready for Jesus' birthday. By our actions, thoughts and prayers, we show God we are thankful that his Son Jesus came to bring love and light into our world.

Jesus brings us love and light not just on Christmas, but on each and every day. Advent is a time for opening our hearts to the coming of Jesus—at Christmas and all year long.

 **Let's Pray!**

In Advent, Lord Jesus, we wait and pray. We know your birthday is near. Help us to get ready by making room for you in our hearts. Help us to also remember that you will come again at the end of time—just as you promised. We love you, Jesus! Amen.

Let's Do a Project!

1

Decorate a small box to use as a "manger." Keep the manger in your room. For every good and kind deed you do or sacrifice you make, place a piece of straw inside. (**Hint:** If you don't have any real straw, you can cut up thin strips of paper to use as straw.) Watch the straw pile grow with all your good deeds, making a nice soft place for Jesus to lay on Christmas Day!

2

Make a mini Advent Wreath for your room. (You might need some grown-ups to help you.) Use a sturdy paper plate or a large plastic coffee can top (about 6½ inches in diameter). Cut a 3-inch circle out of the middle to make the wreath shape.

Next cut three purple and one pink square (about 4 in x 5½ in) out of construction paper. Roll them along the 4-inch side and tape or glue them into candle shapes. Glue small pieces (1 in x 2 in, crumpled together at the bottom) of yellow tissue paper inside the tops of the candles to make the flames.

Cut five ⅜-of-an-inch slits in the bottoms of the candles. Open out the slits to make a base for the candle. Glue or tape the candles to the base, spacing them equally. Wrap green yarn around the base to create an evergreen wreath. If you'd like, add construction paper leaves to the wreath.

Keep the wreath in your bedroom to remind you each day that we are celebrating the season of Advent.

3

Advent is a time to remember how Mary and Joseph got ready for Jesus' birth. With your parents' permission, help a family less fortunate than yours by gathering together baby supplies, such as diapers, wipes, bottles, baby powder and cream, formula and other small infant items. Put them together in a nice bag or bundle. Give the "Get-Ready-for-Baby" bundle to a local food bank, soup kitchen or shelter for a needy mother-to-be.

Turn to page 95 for a picture to color!

Feast of the Immaculate Conception

December 8

Mary was a special young woman. She lived in Israel about 2000 years ago. She was a lot like the other young women of her time. But God had a special plan for Mary. God chose her to be the mother of his Son Jesus. Because of this, God gave Mary the gift of being conceived without original sin. This is what the words "Immaculate Conception" mean. Mary was especially good and pure because she never sinned. She obeyed God every day and was loving and kind to others.

One day, the angel Gabriel visited Mary at her house. He brought her the wonderful news that God had chosen her to be the mother of his Son!

On the Feast of the Immaculate Conception, we listen to the story of Gabriel's visit to Mary. We hear how she praised God for his goodness and thanked him for all he did for her.

We can try to be like Mary. We can ask God to fill us with *grace*, his very own life. We can try never to offend God by what we think, say or do.

Let's Pray!

Dear Mary, you give us the example of a pure and a holy life. Today we celebrate the special gift and privilege God gave you. God kept you free from original sin from the very first moment of your life. God did this because he had chosen you to be the mother of his Son. What a wonderful gift! Help us to love and obey God as you always did, Mary. Amen.

Let's Do a Project!

1

The *rosary* is a special prayer in which we remember things that happened in the lives of Jesus and Mary. We pray it using beads called *rosary beads*. Make your own rosary beads using yarn and pasta shapes or beads, following the diagram below as a model (or ask your parents to get you a rosary).

Learn to pray the rosary today, as the diagram shows you. (You can also ask your parents or teachers for help.) Then hang your rosary beads in a

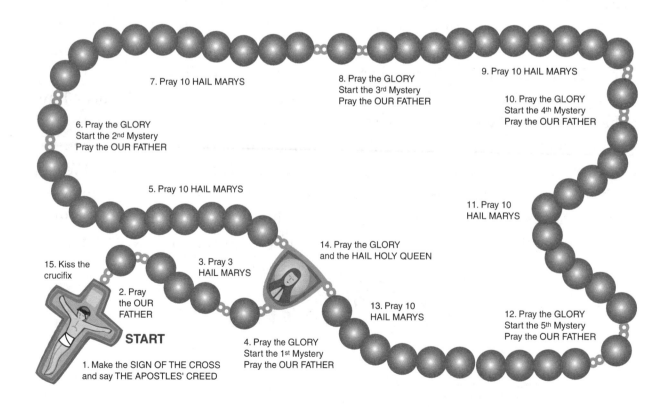

7. Pray 10 HAIL MARYS

8. Pray the GLORY
Start the 3rd Mystery
Pray the OUR FATHER

9. Pray 10 HAIL MARYS

10. Pray the GLORY
Start the 4th Mystery
Pray the OUR FATHER

6. Pray the GLORY
Start the 2nd Mystery
Pray the OUR FATHER

5. Pray 10 HAIL MARYS

14. Pray the GLORY
and the HAIL HOLY QUEEN

11. Pray 10
HAIL MARYS

15. Kiss the
crucifix

3. Pray 3
HAIL MARYS

2. Pray
the OUR
FATHER

13. Pray 10
HAIL MARYS

12. Pray the GLORY
Start the 5th Mystery
Pray the OUR FATHER

START

4. Pray the GLORY
Start the 1st Mystery
Pray the OUR FATHER

1. Make the SIGN OF THE CROSS
and say THE APOSTLES' CREED

place where you'll see them often. They will remind you to pray the rosary, thinking about the lives of Jesus and Mary.

2

The Feast of the Immaculate Conception teaches us that God kept Mary free from sin from the moment of her conception because she was to be the mother of his Son.

Even though we are not free from sin as Mary was, we can try day by day to become better and holier.

Think of something you do that is not pleasing to God. It might be telling little lies or answering your parents or teachers back. Promise God that you'll try to give up this bad habit. Write your promise down so that you can read it once in a while. Then ask Mary to help you keep your good resolution.

3

In 1858 Mary appeared many times to Saint Bernadette Soubirous in the village of Lourdes, France. At first, Bernadette didn't know it was the Blessed Mother. And so she asked the Lady her name. Mary finally answered, "I am the Immaculate Conception."

Read a library book on the story of Mary and Saint Bernadette at Lourdes, or have someone read you the story. Then tell it to a friend.

4

Ask your parents to get you a Miraculous Medal (the medal of the Immaculate Conception) at a religious goods store. Then ask your priest to bless it. Wear it to remind you of Mary, our Blessed Mother, and of her special love for you.

Turn to page 97 for a picture to color!

Christmas

December 25

Children and even grownups look forward to their birthdays. They wait for them with excitement every year. Now imagine a whole world filled with children and grownups waiting for one special birthday—the birthday of their Savior!

Over 2000 years ago, many people were waiting for the Savior God had promised to send. The Savior would come to earth to save all people from their sins. He would teach them how to live and love. The Savior would be God's own Son.

One day a star appeared in the sky over a stable in Bethlehem. The angels sang to the shepherds in the fields. Then the shepherds knew that God's promise had come true. Jesus, the Savior, had been born!

We learn a lot from the way in which Jesus was born. He was not born in a palace or a warm house, but in a place where animals were kept. The first people to hear the news of his birth were not kings or important people, but poor, humble shepherds working in the muddy fields. Jesus did not come as a strong and powerful king, but as a tiny, helpless baby. Jesus shows us that we don't need to be rich, important or powerful to be part of his kingdom. He comes for the smallest and neediest.

We celebrate Christmas like other birthdays, with our family and friends, both at church and at home. We are joyful that Jesus came into our world.

On Christmas we gather at church with all of God's family to thank God for giving us Jesus. During Mass, we listen to the story of Jesus' birth. We sing Christmas carols of joy. We praise and thank God our Father for sending us Jesus his Son.

At Christmastime our church is filled with special decorations like evergreen trees and wreaths, poinsettias and red ribbons. But the most important decoration of all is the nativity scene. There we see statues of Baby Jesus with Mary, Joseph, the shepherds and the animals all around him. The nativity scene teaches us about the simple way that Jesus came into the world.

Giving gifts is another way of celebrating Christmas. God began by giving us his greatest gift, Jesus. Then Jesus gave us his gifts of love and taught us how to live. On Christmas we give gifts to show our love and appreciation for others.

The Christmas season is a good time to remember to share with those who have less than we do. It's a good time to bring joy and friendship to those who are sad or lonely. Many churches set up a Giving Tree with names of children or elderly people who won't receive many gifts. We may choose a name from the tree and give that person a gift. One of Jesus' most important lessons is that we should care for each other, at Christmas and all year long.

At Christmas, we remember to say thank you to everyone who makes our life good for us. We thank everyone for his or her gifts. And most of all, we say "Thank you, God!" for all the gifts he has given us, especially for Jesus who was born on Christmas.

 ## Let's Pray!

Dear Jesus, on Christmas Day we celebrate your birth. You came from God into our world and blessed us with your life and love. You came for all. You love us all. This makes us so happy! Help us to remember that on Christmas *you* are God's most special gift to us! Amen.

Let's Do a Project!

1

Make greeting cards that show the true meaning of Christmas. (**Hint:** You might want to ask a grownup to help you with this project.)

Fold two sheets of construction paper in half. Cut an opening in one of the sheets to make a flap as shown in the diagram. Next glue the two pieces of construction paper together. Make sure the sheet with the cut-out flap is on the **outside**. Don't glue down the flap section.

On the outside of the flap, draw a picture (or cut one out of a magazine or old holiday card and glue it on the flap) of a non-religious image of Christmas (like Santa Claus, a snowman, a Christmas tree or Christmas presents).

On the inside of the flap, draw or glue a picture showing the true meaning of Christmas (for example, Jesus in the stable, the star of Bethlehem or the angels announcing Jesus' birth).

On the blank space under the flap, write a message like "May Jesus, the true center of Christmas, fill you with his love and joy!"

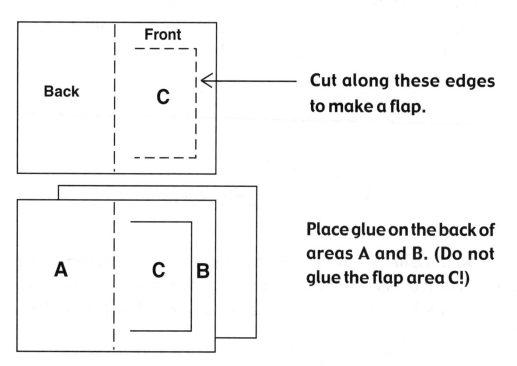

Cut along these edges to make a flap.

Place glue on the back of areas A and B. (Do not glue the flap area C!)

Give the cards to your family and friends before Christmas.

2

Do a special project with your family to share the joy of Christmas with those who are less fortunate. Ask each member of the family to buy, wrap and place under the Christmas tree an extra gift (it could be a toy, food, clothing or household item). Label it "To a Friend of Jesus." On Christmas morning, gather all the extra gifts together in a gift bag and bring them to your church or a local soup kitchen or shelter to be shared with a family in need.

3

Make a nativity scene suncatcher for your house or as a gift for someone special. Cut out nativity pictures from old Christmas cards. Cut two pieces of wax paper the size that you would like your suncatcher to be. Position the nativity pictures on one sheet of wax paper and cover with the second sheet. Lay a piece of newspaper or a towel on top of the wax papers. With the help of a grownup, press gently with a warm iron.

Allow the suncatcher to cool before moving it. Then make two frames with construction paper or craft sticks. Glue a frame to each side of the suncatcher and glue a loop of yarn or string to the top center of the frame. Hang the suncatcher with the picture facing you.

4

If you have the Internet at home, use it to tell someone about the *true* story of Christmas. At the end of your message, type this line: "Pass this message on to someone else!"

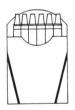 **Turn to page 99 for a picture to color!**

Feast of the Holy Family

The Sunday after Christmas

(When Christmas is on a Sunday, this feast is celebrated on December 30.)

Jesus is the Son of God, but he lived on earth just like any little boy or girl. First he was a tiny baby, then he learned to walk and talk. Jesus liked to play and listen to stories and watch everything around him. He grew bigger and stronger. He went to Hebrew school to learn to read the Scriptures.

Jesus lived in a house with his mother Mary and Joseph, who was his father on earth. Jesus loved to hug and kiss them. He did little chores around the house for Mary. He helped Joseph in his carpenter's shop. Even though Jesus was the Son of God, he always obeyed Mary and Joseph. He listened to them when they taught him things.

On this Feast of the Holy Family, we learn about Jesus' family on earth. Jesus was happy to be a part of his family.

Each of us has a special family, too. We remember that we are blessed to have our family. We thank God who gave us our parents and brothers and sisters. We thank him for all our family members, even those who are separated from us. Jesus wants us to respect the members of our family, and treat each of them with kindness and consideration. He also teaches us to obey those who care for us. When we do as Jesus shows us, our families are blessed.

Besides our own families, we belong to another great big family—God's family.

God's family is made up of all the people he has created. There are some who are like us and some who are different. Even if someone looks different, we love and care for that person because we know that we all have the same Heavenly Father. We are all children of God.

On the Feast of the Holy Family, we thank God for families—Jesus' family on earth, our own families, and the big family of God.

Let's Pray!

Jesus, you were once a boy, a young person just like me. You were cared for by your family, which we honor today. Thank you for showing me how to love, obey, and honor those who care for me. Please help me to be like you, Jesus. I want to do all I can to make my home and family a loving, happy, and helping one. Amen.

Let's Do a Project!

1

Hold a "Happy Holy Family" party with your family. Decorate a room with signs that say things like "Thank You for Our Family, God!" "We Are Blessed!" "Love One Another" and "Let's Celebrate Our Family!" Bake a cake and write on it "Happy Holy Family Day!" At the celebration, have each member of the family share their thoughts about what made Jesus' family holy and how your family can be holy. Join hands at the end of the party, and promise to do all you can to be a "Holy Family" like Jesus, Mary and Joseph.

2

Families come in all shapes and sizes! Draw a poster of your own family. Don't forget to write the name of each person in the drawing. Then show it to the members of your family. Share what you think makes your family different and special. Every family can be holy and blessed when it's filled with love and the spirit of Jesus!

3

Make a three-dimensional miniature scene from the life of the boy Jesus. Create your scene on the inside bottom of a shoebox, so that when it is standing, the sides of the box form a frame. Use materials such as construction paper, cardboard, modeling clay, pieces of wood or small branches, etc., to create your scene and make the little figures. The scene can be from Jesus' everyday life with Mary and Joseph, or it can show one of the special events of Jesus' childhood.

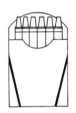

Turn to page 101 for a picture to color!

Feast of Mary, Mother of God

January 1

(Option: Mass for Peace and Justice)

God chose Mary, a young Jewish woman who was loving and kind, to be the mother of his Son. God knew that she would be a good mother for Jesus.

On January 1, we join together to honor Mary who is the best model for all mothers and all Christians.

Mary's life as a mother was like the lives of many mothers. It was filled with love and joy, but there were also difficulties, sacrifices and sorrows.

The days before Jesus was born were not easy for Mary. She had to travel with her husband Joseph through the desert to Bethlehem. Since they could not find a warm and comfortable room, they slept in a cold shelter for animals. Jesus was born there.

Then Mary was afraid for her baby when Joseph received a message from God that King Herod wanted to kill Jesus. Joseph obeyed God, escaping with Mary and Jesus to the country of Egypt. They lived in that country far from home until Herod died. Finally, God sent an angel to tell them to return home to Israel.

As Jesus grew, Mary cared for him just as our mothers care for us. She fed and dressed him. She helped him with his lessons. She played with him.

When Jesus grew up, Mary saw him leave home. He had to go to many places and see many people to teach them about God his Father. Mary missed him while he was gone, but she knew his work had to be done. She encouraged Jesus to be the best teacher he could be.

Mary's biggest sacrifice came when Jesus was put to death. She wanted to protect him from his enemies and save him. But she realized that Jesus had to complete his mission and die to save us from our sins.

Jesus loved his mother Mary. We learn from his example how to treat our own mothers—with love, gratefulness and respect. Jesus shares his mother with us, too. Mary loves us and keeps us close to Jesus.

January 1 is also a day to celebrate a Mass for Peace and Justice.

The first day of the new year is a time when we promise to try to make our lives better. We try to have peace in our families and share what we have with others.

It's also a good time for our Church to find ways to make things better. We pray for our world. There are many people to help and problems to solve.

There are people who do not get along well with one another. They may be unfriendly or unhelpful, and may even fight with each other sometimes. When armies attack each other with guns and bombs, it's called a war. People are hurt and killed and life is very unhappy.

God does not want people to fight, or countries to be at war. Instead, he wants us to love each other. He wants us to accept our differences and learn to get along with each other.

God asks us to say we're sorry when we hurt someone, and to forgive those who hurt us. He tells us to live as a community of people who love and care for one another. At Mass on January 1, we can pray for peace everywhere—at home, in our town or city, in our country and around the world.

At this Mass, we also pray for *justice*. To practice justice means to respect the rights that God gave each of us when he created us. We are all children of God, and God gave the world and everything in it to his children. We must be sure that everyone has a fair share of these good things. Rich countries must make sure that poor countries are treated with justice.

God gives us the job of bringing peace and justice to our world. When we attend a Mass for Peace and Justice, we pray that God will give us the courage and strength to do the job.

Let's Pray!

Heavenly Father, today is the first day of a new year. It's also the day when we honor in a special way Mary, the Mother of God. We thank Mary today for bringing Jesus into our world. We pray that this year we will all get closer to you. We pray that people all over the world will live in peace, and that there will be justice for everyone. Amen.

Let's Do a Project!

1

God asked Mary to do something very special when he asked her to be the mother of Jesus. Mary shows us how important mothers really are.

As we honor Mary, the Mother of God today, it's a good time to honor our own mother, too. Make a bouquet of love notes for her. Cut 3-inch hearts out of pink construction paper. Write on each heart a message of love or gratitude or something that you will do to help her.

Cut green pipe cleaners into lengths from 6 to 10 inches. Glue each heart to a pipe cleaner. Decorate an empty margarine container with construction paper or pretty giftwrap. Glue a piece of Styrofoam to the bottom of the container. Stick the pipe cleaner flowers into the pot.

When you give the bouquet to your mother or special caretaker, tell her you are honoring her in memory of Mary, the mother of Jesus. On the days that follow, help her by doing the things you wrote on the flowers.

2

Our country is blessed in so many ways. We have beautiful land, many natural resources, and peace and freedom for all. But we must remember the other children of God all over the earth. Some live in countries where there are fewer resources or where there is no peace and justice.

Make a Chain of World Peace. Cut 8½ in x 11½ in strips of colored paper. On each strip, write the name of a country. Think of as many as you can on your own, then use a reference book or the help of a grownup to add as many others as you can.

Glue or tape the strips together, linking them with one another into a chain. Hang your Chain of World Peace in your home or classroom and say a prayer asking God to help all people to be like this chain, held together by love and support for one another.

3

Knowing about problems can help us to understand them and find ways to solve them. Do the following project with your family or classmates to learn about conflict and war around the world.

Divide into groups and ask each group to find out about a part of the world that is not at peace. Then, each group can share with the others what they have learned. Afterward, have a brainstorming session to come up with ways to bring peace to those places.

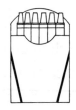

Turn to page 103 for a picture to color!

Feast of the Epiphany

The Sunday between January 2 and January 8

THREE WISE MEN CAME...

(In countries where it is a holy day of obligation, Epiphany is celebrated on January 6.)

Soon after Jesus was born, he had special visitors. They were three wise men who came from faraway lands. According to what has been passed down to us, their names were Gaspar, Melchior and Balthasar. They brought Jesus gifts of gold, frankincense and myrrh. These men were astrologers (people who studied the stars) and they had seen a new star in the sky. They followed that star to find Jesus, the Savior of the world.

The wise men, who are also called the Magi, were very intelligent and wealthy. They lived in palaces filled with riches and wore clothing of the finest fabrics. They wore crowns of gold and jewels on their heads. People could easily see that they were powerful and important.

Instead, Jesus was poor. He was born in a stable and his bed was the lamb's manger. Jesus' clothes were plain pieces of cloth, and he wore no crown. Jesus was simple and humble. Nobody could tell just by looking at him that he was an important baby and even a powerful king!

But somehow, the three wise men knew that Jesus was really the greatest king ever born. Somehow they could see the promise of God in this poor little baby. They knew that this baby would do more to change the world than any other king who had ever lived or would ever live.

Jesus is the greatest king because he brought us the hope of going to heaven, where all may go after living a life of love and goodness on earth.

The wise men help us to understand another important thing about Jesus our Savior and King. The wise men lived in different countries. They spoke different languages. They had different skin colors and practiced dif- ferent religions. They were not like the people in Jesus' family. But Jesus was born for the wise men, too. Jesus came to save everyone, not just people like himself. For this reason, we know that God loves all people equally. He wants us to do the same thing.

We celebrate the Feast of the Epiphany by remembering the long search and journey of the wise men. We also learn from their example to look for Jesus where we least expect him— in all people around us, especially in those who are poor and humble.

Let's Pray!

Jesus, when you were born, the shepherds nearby rejoiced. But far away, three wise men knew that you were special, too. I pray that I will be like them. Help me to remember that you came to bring God's love and salvation to everyone. You are King of all people, both great and small. Help me to share your love with those who might be different from me in some way. Let me see your face in every person. Let me remember that we are all one in you. Amen.

Let's Do a Project!

1

The three wise men found Jesus in a poor stable. They saw their King in a helpless, humble baby. We need to see Jesus in the most helpless and humble people around us. Find a way to help these people, by bringing the light of

Jesus' star into their world. Visit a nursing home, help serve food at a soup kitchen, or help sponsor a child in a poor country. Join a ministry at your church that helps others. Do this with your family or class.

2

Make a star suncatcher to hang in your home on the Epiphany. Cut out two 10 in x 10 in squares of clear contact paper. Sprinkle gold glitter onto the sticky side of one sheet of contact paper. Lay the second sheet of contact paper on it. Lightly trace and then cut a star shape out of the square. Punch a hole in the top of the star and thread a piece of yellow yarn or clear nylon thread through the hole. Hang the star in a window or in a spot in your home where all can see it. Make a pledge to follow the star by spreading the love of Jesus today and every day.

3

The wise men brought Jesus gifts of gold, frankincense and myrrh. These gifts honored Jesus as King, God and man. Think of three gifts that you would like to give Jesus. They could be acts of service, or ways that you will try to be more like him. Write each one down on a piece of paper. Place each paper in a small gift box and wrap the boxes. Place the gifts before the nativity scene at home or in church. Remember to give the gifts you've promised to Jesus!

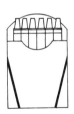

Turn to page 105 for a picture to color!

Feast of the Baptism of the Lord

The Sunday after January 6

This is My Beloved Son...

After he grew up, Jesus' cousin John the Baptist began speaking to the people about the coming of Jesus. He asked them to prepare the way for the Lord. People came to John to tell their sins and to be washed clean. John baptized them in the Jordan River.

One day, when Jesus was about thirty years old, he went to John. He wanted to be baptized. Because Jesus is God, he didn't need to be washed clean of sin, but he wanted to give us this good example.

At first, John didn't want to baptize Jesus. He wanted Jesus to baptize him instead. But Jesus said they should do what God asked of them. So John and Jesus went into the river, and John baptized his cousin. At that moment, a dove appeared over Jesus' head. This was a sign that the Holy Spirit was there. Then God's voice was heard saying, "This is my beloved Son with whom I am very pleased!"

When we were baptized, we were washed clean of sin and we became members of Jesus' Church. We know that God loves *us* and is pleased with us, too!

Let's Pray!

Jesus, your baptism shows us many things. It shows that you wanted to follow God's plan for you and do everything he asked. It shows that God the Father was very pleased with you. It especially shows us that we should be humble and kind and always ready to do God's will. Help us to be more like you every day, Jesus! Amen.

Let's Do a Project!

1

Baptisms are celebrated either at Sunday Mass or at a ceremony just for the families of the babies being baptized. Baptisms of grownups are celebrated at the Easter Vigil liturgy. Try to attend a baptism. Pay attention to the different parts of the ceremony. After the baptism, draw a picture of what you saw.

2

With your family or class, act out the baptism of Jesus. Read the story from the Gospel (Mt 3:13–17) and write lines for each of the characters. Assign the parts of a narrator, John the Baptist, Jesus, the voice of God, and the Holy Spirit. End by saying a prayer to thank God for your own baptism.

3

Make a baptism water globe. Find a plastic cross or crucifix that's small enough to fit inside a small glass jar (like a baby food jar). With a grownup, use a hot-glue gun to glue the cross to the inside bottom of the jar. Fill the jar almost to the top with water. Spoon in some large-sized gold or silver glitter or small sequins. Put epoxy glue around the opening of the jar and the lid. Screw on the top and allow to dry. When you shake your baptism globe, let it remind you of God's grace that cleansed you and freed you from sin at your baptism.

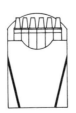

Turn to page 107 for a picture to color!

Lent

Prayer
+ Service
+ Sacrifice

Lent occurs in winter in many parts of the world. The days are cold. Darkness comes early in the evening. The trees are bare and the ground is brown and lifeless. Lent lasts for forty days.

Near the end of Lent, spring arrives. The cold and dark days are over, and signs of new life appear. The days are brighter and longer. Leaves are budding, and flowers are poking through the soil.

Lent is like springtime for our Church and our souls. It gets us ready for the new life and happiness of Easter. It's a quiet and prayerful time when we try to become better followers of Jesus. During Lent, we try to become closer to God. We get ready to celebrate Holy Week and Easter, when we remember Jesus' death and resurrection.

There are three important ways to grow closer to God during Lent. They are: 1. prayer, 2. sacrifice and 3. service.

Prayer is speaking with God and listening to him speak to us. When we get into the habit of praying more each day, we realize how close God is to each of us. We learn how much he loves us and how he would like us to live our lives. God is our most forgiving, understanding and gentle Father. He is always ready to help us. During Lent, we tell God often that we are sorry when we haven't been as good as we could have been. As we try harder each day to be loving and kind, prayer is like God's loving arms around us, protecting, helping and encouraging us.

To *sacrifice* means to give up something we like. We may give up something we like to eat or do as a way of making more room for God in our lives. The Church asks all those who are fourteen years old or older to make the sacrifice of not eating any meat on Ash Wednesday, Good Friday and all the Fridays of Lent. We can eat fish, eggs, or other food on those days. Catholics between the ages of eighteen and fifty-nine are also asked to *fast* on Ash Wednesday and Good Friday. This means that they may only eat one main meal and two smaller meals as a way of doing penance and offering a sacrifice to God.

God gave us all the wonderful things we enjoy. When we go without them for a while, it makes us appreciate God's gifts more than ever. Being thankful to God is an important part of Lent.

When we make sacrifices and give up things, we can also find new ways to help and bring happiness to others. This is called *service*. While we may not give away the candy or ice cream that we don't eat, we may share other kinds of food with the hungry. We can give our time to an organization that helps people in need. We can find many ways to help others in our neighborhoods, schools and in our own families.

Our church shows the quiet mood of Lent. The chasuble, or outer vestment the priest wears, is purple. The altar might also be covered with a deep purple cloth. The purple color reminds us that we should be sorry for our sins and make some little sacrifices as we get ready for Easter. During Lent we do not sing "Alleluia," which means "Praise God." This makes singing "Alleluia" again on Easter even more joyful.

Ash Wednesday

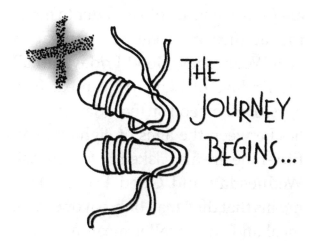

THE JOURNEY BEGINS...

Ash Wednesday is the first day of Lent. When we go to church on this day, the priest marks a cross on our foreheads with ashes. The ashes come from the palms used on last year's Palm Sunday. Just before Lent, these palms are gathered, burned and blessed.

What does the cross of ashes mean? It is a sign that we are ready to begin the season of Lent. It reminds us that during this time we want to be especially sorry for our sins and grow closer to God.

As the priest marks our forehead with the cross of ashes he says, "Turn away from sin and be faithful to the Gospel," or "Remember, man, you are dust and to dust you will return."

What does the priest mean when he says we will return to dust? Think of your body. We each have a body that needs care. We eat to stay healthy. We clean and dress ourselves. We sleep to get energy. We use our bodies to live—to work, to play and to move around.

When we die, whether we are buried or cremated, our bodies finally turn to dust. The ashes we receive on Ash Wednesday remind us to live a good life and to be sorry for the sins we commit, because this life is short and some day all of us will die.

But we are more than just our bodies. Each of us is made up of both a body and soul. Our soul does not stop living when our body does. If we do

34

as the priest tells us on Ash Wednesday, if we turn away from sin, and try to live by Jesus' Gospel, our soul will go to heaven when our life on earth ends. At the end of the world, God will unite our soul with our body again and we will live forever with him!

Let's Pray!

Jesus, today we begin the season of Lent. We wear the sign of your cross on our foreheads. Let this cross remind us and everyone who sees us that we love and follow you. Watch over us during our forty days of waiting and of growing in your love. On this first day of Lent, help us to think of some ways that we can grow closer to you—in prayer, in sacrifice, and in service. Amen.

Let's Do a Project!

1

Draw a picture of yourself with the cross of ashes on your forehead. Around your face, write down the things that you want to do this Lent to come closer to God. (**Hint:** It's better to choose only a few things that you really can do. If you write down too many, you might not do any!)

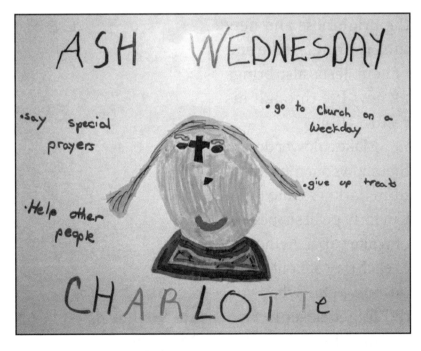

Hang your self-portrait in your room to remind you each day of your lenten resolutions.

2

Set up a prayer corner in your room, a special place where you can spend a little extra time talking with God during Lent. You may want to put a crucifix or a picture of Jesus in your prayer corner. If you have a Bible, a prayer book or a rosary, you can put them there, too. You might also ask your Mom for a pillow or a small rug that you can sit or kneel on while you are praying.

3

The forty days of Lent move us from the dark of winter into the brightness and new life of spring. At the end of Lent, Jesus also brings us new life through his resurrection.

Make a flower design that shows our movement from darkness into light. Cut forty petal shapes out of white paper. At the end of each day of Lent, write on one petal what you did to get closer to God that day. (Remember that prayer, small sacrifices, and acts of love and service to others are special ways to grow closer to God during Lent.)

Color the edge of the petal with the colors listed below:

Days 1–5: dark brown
Days 6–10: light brown
Days 11–15: dark purple
Days 16–20: dark blue
Days 21–25: dark green
Days 26–30: light green
Days 31–40: the bright colors of spring flowers—light purple, light blue, pink, yellow.

Each day, glue a petal to a poster board in the shape of a flower, beginning at the center with the dark brown and spiraling around as Lent passes.

Print in purple letters "MY LENTEN JOURNEY" along the top of the poster. Along the bottom, print "From darkness into light!" Print "darkness" in brown and "light" in yellow.

At the end of Lent, draw a stem with leaves to finish the flower.

4

Choose a favorite TV program or video game and decide to give it up for Lent, or at least on the weekdays of Lent. Instead, read a book of lives of the saints, or a story of a good person who can inspire you.

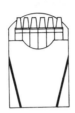

Turn to page 109 for a picture to color!

Feast of Saint Joseph, the Husband of Mary

March 19

Joseph was the husband of Mary and the foster father of Jesus. We honor him because he played a very important role in their lives, protecting and caring for them both.

Joseph and Mary were not yet married when Mary learned that she was to be the mother of Jesus. Joseph could have gotten angry and broken off the engagement, but he wanted to protect Mary from being hurt. An angel spoke to him in a dream and told him that the Holy Spirit made it possible for Mary to be the mother of God. Joseph believed the angel and married Mary.

Later, Mary and Joseph went to Bethlehem, where Jesus was born. Again, an angel spoke to Joseph in a dream. The angel told Joseph to protect Jesus from the evil King Herod, who wanted him killed. He told Joseph to take Jesus to another land where he would be safe. Once more, Joseph believed the angel. To protect Jesus, Joseph took his family to the country of Egypt, where they stayed for several years.

Joseph was visited by an angel one last time. The angel said it was safe for him to bring his family home. With great joy, they returned to their own country and made their home in Nazareth.

Joseph was a man of great faith. God asked things of him that were hard to understand and do. Yet Joseph trusted in God and always obeyed him. He was a model husband and father because he protected and cared for his family. He was a simple man who worked as a carpenter. We learn from Joseph how to find greatness in simply obeying God and working hard.

The stories of Joseph's life show us that a follower of God does not have to be a famous hero with an exciting life to do God's work. Sometimes, we do his work simply by being a good brother or sister, or mother or father, who loves and cares for the other family members.

Joseph is the patron saint of the Church, fathers, families and carpenters.

Let's Pray!

Heavenly Father, today we thank you for the kind foster father you gave your Son Jesus. Joseph always obeyed you, loved his family and lived his faith. We thank you, Saint Joseph, for taking good care of Mary and Jesus. Help us to love and obey God just as you did. Amen.

Let's Do a Project!

1

Joseph was a very good husband and father. Make a booklet showing some of the many ways he cared for Jesus and Mary. Use pieces of white cardboard or construction paper. Draw pictures and write several words describing the scenes on each of the pages.

Make a cover page with the title, "Joseph, the Husband of Mary." Then punch three holes along the left-hand side of the pages. Cut three 5-inch strands of yarn and string them through the holes to join the pages into a booklet. Share your booklet with your family and friends.

2

Joseph was a carpenter who used wood to build things. Jesus learned from him how to build with wood, too. It is an important symbol that Jesus was a carpenter. Not only did Jesus build with wood, he also built the family of God by teaching people about God our Father and showing them how to love each other.

Build a little church out of wood. Use sticks that you gather outdoors, craft sticks or other small pieces of wood. Glue or tie them together to form three sides and two roof pieces. Attach them together in the shape of a church. Make a steeple in the shape of a cross for the top. Display the church in your room to remind you that like Jesus and Joseph the carpenters, you can help build God's Church through your words and deeds!

3

Think of someone you know who is a good husband and father. Think of the ways that he is like Joseph. Write a letter to him explaining how he reminds you of Saint Joseph, and thank him for his good example.

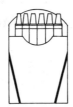

**Turn to page 111
for a picture
to color!**

Feast of the Annunciation

March 25

YES, LORD

One day, an angel visited Mary and told her important news. The angel's name was Gabriel, and the news was that God had chosen her to be the mother of his Son!

Mary was only a young teenager, and not yet married to Joseph. How could she become a mother? She asked the angel.

Gabriel told her that the Holy Spirit would make it possible. Mary didn't really understand, but she accepted Gabriel's words and God's special plan for her. This is a won-derful example of Mary's faith in God.

Mary chose to obey God's will and said "Yes" when he asked her to become the mother of his Son. She was surprised to be chosen. Maybe she also worried that it might be hard to be the mother of God's Son—but she still said, "Yes!" Mary trusted that God would help her.

On the Feast of the Annunciation, a word which means "the telling," we remember Mary and try to be like her. If we ask her to, Mary will help us to always say "Yes!" to God as she did.

Let's Pray!

Dear Mary, today we remember how God sent an angel to tell you that he had chosen you to be the mother of his Son. When you heard this news, you gladly said, "Yes!" Help us, Mary, to say "Yes!" to whatever God asks us to do. Amen.

Let's Do a Project!

1

Mary prayed a special prayer in response to the message of the angel Gabriel. This prayer is called the Magnificat. Think of some of the good things God has done for you and your family, and then pray the Magnificat to thank him.

A Young Person's Magnificat

My soul sings
how great is the Lord!
My spirit finds joy
in God who saves me,
for he has looked down on me,
his humble child.
From now on, all people
will call me blessed,
for God has done
great things for me.
Holy is God's name
and he is kind to all his people.
God has shown his power
and cared for the poor and lowly.
He has come to help his people
as he promised long ago!
Amen.

2

Mary gladly said "Yes!" when the angel told her what God was asking her to do. Think of things that God might be asking YOU to do—for example, play with a classmate who doesn't have many friends, give up a weekend afternoon to visit the elderly in a nursing home, or do your chores without complaining.

Make a special effort to say "Yes!" to opportunities like these, with the same joy and praise that Mary had when she said "Yes!" to God.

3

Draw a picture of the beautiful scene of the angel Gabriel's annunciation to Mary. Imagine how Mary felt when she heard the news that she was to be the mother of God's own Son! All around your picture, write down words to describe Mary's reaction and feelings. At the bottom of the picture, write "Thank you, Mary, for saying Yes!"

Turn to page 113 for a picture to color!

Passion Sunday

Also called Palm Sunday

Think of the last time you went to a parade. Remember the excitement of gathering along the street with hundreds of other people. Remember hearing the sounds of music, sirens, and joyful voices, and watching the fantastic show.

That's something of what it was like in Jerusalem on Palm Sunday. But on that day the people weren't lined up in the streets to see marching bands, balloons and flower-filled floats. Instead, they were waiting for one simple man riding on a donkey. All the excitement that day was about Jesus!

When Jesus rode into the big city of Jerusalem, there were crowds of people who loved him and knew he was someone special. They greeted him by waving palm branches and laying their coats on the ground ahead of him. It was a day of great triumph for Jesus.

But now we know that Palm Sunday was also the beginning of the suffering that would lead to Jesus' death. Some people didn't understand his message. They were afraid and jealous of his power over the crowds of believers. They were already planning how to get rid of Jesus.

On Palm Sunday, which is also called Passion Sunday, we listen to the long story of the passion (the suffering and death) of Jesus. Hearing this story helps us to prepare to celebrate Holy Week, the time when we remember the last days of Jesus' life on earth.

The priest blesses palm branches at Mass, in memory of the palm branches the people waved when Jesus rode into Jerusalem. We bring them home from church to put near our crucifixes. (A crucifix is a cross that has an image of Jesus on it.) These branches will remind us all year long that Jesus is our King and that we should always praise him. Some of the palm branches blessed today will be burned in one year to be used as the ashes for next Ash Wednesday.

The priest's chasuble (outer vestment) and the altar decorations today are red, which is a kingly color. On this feast we join in the words of praise sung by the people of Jerusalem many years ago: "Hosanna to the Son of David! Blest is he who comes in the name of the Lord. Hosanna in the highest!"

The word "Hosanna" is a cry of praise to God. We say "Hosanna" on Palm Sunday and at every Mass. We thank Jesus for being our Savior and our King.

Let's Pray!

Jesus, we sing Hosanna to you today. Though you rode on a donkey and were humble and poor, we know you are our King. Thank you for showing us that a king can be kind and gentle. Thank you for teaching us that a great person does not have to be rich. You are King of all people everywhere. Help us to praise you every day of the year! Amen.

Let's Do a Project!

1

Prepare for Holy Week and Easter by making a picture display. Cut out five pieces of white cardboard that are about 5 in x 7 in. Cut two holes on each of the long sides.

On each piece of cardboard, draw a picture of Jesus on one of the days of Holy Week: Palm Sunday, Holy Thursday, Good Friday and Holy Saturday. On the fifth piece, draw a picture of Jesus on Easter Sunday. Write the name of the day on each picture.

Next cut out eight strands of red yarn about 5 inches long. When the pictures are done, put them in order and tie them together by stringing the yarn through the holes of the pieces next to each other and tying a knot in the back.

When the pieces are strung together, stand them up on a table in your home or on the dresser in your bedroom. As each of the days of Holy Week comes, look at your picture of it and thank Jesus for what he did for us.

2

When you go to church on Palm Sunday, try to bring home several pieces of fresh palm, or a large piece that you can divide. With an older family member, fold a piece or two of palm and place it behind a cross or crucifix that is hanging in your home. If you can, place some behind all of the crucifixes that you have. See where the crucifixes are. When was the last time you stopped to look at and pray in front of a crucifix in your home? If you don't have any crosses or crucifixes at home, this is a good time to make or buy one to hang in a special place.

3

When Jesus rode triumphantly into Jerusalem, it was on a tiny donkey and not on a powerful horse or chariot. This reminds us that he is a King for all, both rich and poor people. If your family has a car, try to do an act of service by asking your parents to give someone in need a ride. It could be an elderly person you know who has no ride to church, or a classmate who has to walk home in the cold or rain.

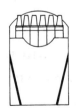

Turn to page 115 for a picture to color!

Holy Thursday

Do this in remembrance of ME

Jesus had eaten many meals with his disciples and friends. But on Holy Thursday he shared the most special meal of all with them. We call that meal the "Last Supper."

Jesus knew that his life on earth would soon be over. But he still had many important lessons and gifts to share with his friends on that Thursday night.

While they were at table, Jesus took a bowl of water and a towel. He went around and washed the feet of each of his disciples. Jesus did this to show us that no person is greater than another person. Jesus did this to teach us that we should love other people just as he loves us.

Then Jesus told his disciples not to be worried and upset that he would leave them. He was just going ahead of them to prepare their places with God in heaven. Jesus promised them that they would see each other again and live together in heaven forever. Jesus also said that he would send the Holy Spirit to help them do their work on earth.

Finally, he shared the most important gift of all. He took a piece of bread, blessed it, and thanked God for it. "Take and eat; this is my body," he said. Then Jesus took a cup of wine. He blessed it, thanked God for it and said, "Take and drink, this is my blood." The bread and the wine were now Jesus' own Body and Blood! At the Last Supper and at every Mass since then, Jesus shares with us his own Body and Blood. These are the food and drink we need to keep spiritually strong and healthy.

On Holy Thursday, we go to Mass to celebrate the Last Supper. We thank

God in a special way for the gifts of the priesthood and the Holy Eucharist. The priest wears a white chasuble. In our Church, white is the color of purity and joy. The priest may also wash the feet of several men. This reminds us of how Jesus washed his apostles' feet at the Last Supper.

Every time we join in the celebration of Mass, God invites us to share in the Body and Blood of his Son Jesus Christ. During the Eucharistic Prayer, the priest asks God to send the Holy Spirit to change the bread and wine into Jesus' Body and Blood. The Holy Spirit does this. Jesus comes to us when we receive Holy Communion.

Let's Pray!

On this day, Jesus, we remember your Last Supper. At that meal you gave your apostles special food—your Body and Blood. You also give this food to us at every Mass. Thank you, Jesus! Receiving you in Holy Communion helps us to be strong and good. Let us always receive you with love and thanks and praise! Amen.

Let's Do a Project!

1

The scene of the Last Supper is one of the most beautiful in Jesus' life. Draw a picture of how you imagine Jesus looked surrounded by his twelve Apostles. Add one more person to the group—yourself. At the bottom of your picture, write how you would feel if you were

at Jesus' Last Supper. Print "HOLY THURSDAY" at the top of the picture.

2

Read the story of how Jesus washed the apostles' feet at the Last Supper. You'll find it in the Bible in John 13:1–17. Then close your eyes and imagine how the apostles felt. Think of what you can do at home to be of more service to your family. Write down at least three things you could do to be more helpful. Put this note under your pillow so that you can reread it every night.

3

Write your own prayer to thank Jesus for the wonderful gift of his Body and Blood in the Holy Eucharist. Then make the prayer into a bookmark by printing or typing it on a piece of colored construction paper that you've cut to the size you want. Use felt markers to decorate the edges with designs or flowers, or paste a small picture of Jesus on your bookmark. Keep the bookmark in your prayer book or Bible.

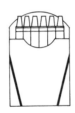

Turn to page 117 for a picture to color!

Good Friday

Good Friday is both a sad and a glad day for us. It's sad because it's the day Jesus was nailed to a wooden cross and died. But it's a glad day because we know that Jesus died out of love for us.

It's hard to imagine that some people didn't love Jesus. He was always so kind, gentle and loving. He never hurt anyone. How could anyone want to kill him?

But some people were jealous of Jesus. They were afraid of the power of his message of love and of his promise of a kingdom in heaven. They couldn't accept Jesus' teachings. And they didn't want others to follow him. So they decided to kill him.

Because Jesus is God, he could have stopped some of the people from putting him to death. But Jesus freely accepted his death on the cross to save us from our sins. He offered his life to God the Father so that we could go to heaven one day.

It's important to go to church on Good Friday to remember how Jesus suffered and died for each one of us. He wanted to show us how much he loves us all! We want to show Jesus that we will stay by his side when others turn against him. We want to thank him for suffering his painful death for us.

On Good Friday we listen to the reading of the passion of our Lord (the Gospel story of Jesus' sufferings and death). We walk to the front of the church to kiss the cross. If we are old enough, we receive Jesus in Holy Communion. The red chasuble the priest wears reminds us of the suffering of Jesus our King.

At home we eat simple food and make sacrifices to share in Jesus' sorrow. (Those who are fourteen years old or more do not eat meat. Those who are between eighteen and fifty-nine years old eat only one main meal.) All day long we try to be quieter and stay close to Jesus in our thoughts and prayers. We learn about true love from Jesus, who loved us so much that he gave his life for us.

After Jesus died on the cross, his friends took him down and wrapped him in a linen cloth. Then they buried him in a cave. A large stone was rolled in front of the entrance of the cave. Jesus' friends were very sad. They thought Jesus had just died like everyone else whom they would never see again. But soon something wonderful would happen. Soon Jesus would rise from the dead as he had promised!

Let's Pray!

Today, Jesus, we celebrate your greatest sacrifice, made out of love for us. You died to give us new life. Thank you, Lord! My heart is sad as I remember your pain. Let me help you carry your cross, Jesus. I can carry your cross by caring about others, by obeying your word, and by trying to always be loving and good. This is what I want to do. Amen.

Let's Do a Project!

1

On Good Friday, we should be quiet and prayerful, remembering how Jesus died. Make a picture like the one below and hang it on the busiest door in your home. Each time you and your family members pass through the door and see the sign, take a moment to remember Jesus and thank him for giving his life for us. Write GOOD FRIDAY at the top of the picture.

I remember you, Jesus!

*Please remember me
when you come into your Kingdom.*

2

Even if you aren't fourteen yet, think of some food you like that you can give up today (like a Coke, or cookies, or even just sugar on your cereal!). Give it up with a smile—for Jesus!

3

With a group of your friends or your class, act out the *Stations of the Cross.*

These are the scenes of Jesus' suffering and death. Form pairs or groups to play the parts in each of the Stations. (**Hint:** You can use the descriptions of the Stations of the Cross in a prayer book to help you act out each scene.) Position each group around the room so that the scenes are in the right order. Invite your family and friends to sit in the center of the room and watch your dramatization of Jesus' passion.

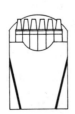

Turn to page 119 for a picture to color!

Holy Saturday

Holy Saturday is the day before Easter Sunday. On this day we remember the time Jesus spent in the tomb before his resurrection on Easter. On this day we pray and prepare our hearts for the great feast of Easter.

If we are old enough, we may also go to the *Easter Vigil*, the special celebration held in our church on the night of Holy Saturday.

Let's Pray!

Today we keep thinking about your wonderful love for us, Jesus. You love us so much that you were willing to die to save us from our sins.

Help us to get our hearts ready for tomorrow—Easter Sunday—the joyful day when we celebrate your rising from the dead! Amen.

Let's Do a Project!

(Since the celebration of Holy Saturday is so closely connected to our Easter Sunday celebration, more projects are listed under Easter.)

1

On Holy Saturday and Easter Sunday, we renew the promises our godparents made for us when we were baptized. Ask your religion teacher or your parents to help you find these baptismal promises in the missalette you use at Mass. Copy down the promises. Draw pictures or designs to go with each one, then staple the pages together to make a little booklet for yourself.

Easter Sunday

The Feast of Jesus' Resurrection

Alleluia
Christ is Risen!

Spring is a time of new life. Leaves reappear on the tree branches. Flowers and plants push their heads up through the chilly soil. The grass grows green and tall again. The air feels fresh and the sun is bright. It's easy to feel excited about the new life of spring.

Easter is a holy day in springtime. It's even more important than the new life of nature. Easter is the greatest of all the holy days in our year with God!

Easter is so important that we begin to celebrate it on the night of Holy Saturday. We do this with a special celebration called the *Easter Vigil*. The word "vigil" means "watch." At the Easter Vigil we are keeping watch or waiting for Easter Sunday.

During the Easter Vigil a big candle called the *paschal candle* is lit and blessed. This candle is a symbol of Jesus, risen from the dead. We listen to many readings from the Bible. At the Easter Vigil new Catholics, both children and grownups, are also welcomed into our Church. This is done in the same way that new members were welcomed into our Church by the very first Christians. These new members receive Baptism, and, if they are old enough, Confirmation and Holy Eucharist, too. Then the Mass continues as usual.

Easter Sunday is the day on which Jesus won a new life for all people by rising from the dead! Jesus' rising is called the *resurrection*. It is amazing and wonderful! We celebrate Jesus' resurrection with great joy and thanks on

Easter Sunday and on every Sunday of the year. And we remember how the resurrection happened....

On the third day after he died and was buried, some women who were Jesus' disciples came to his tomb. An angel appeared to them and told them that Jesus was not there. "He has been raised from the dead, just as he promised!" the angel proclaimed.

The women could see that the tomb was empty. They were frightened and joyful at the same time. They raced to tell the disciples the great news. As they ran, Jesus suddenly stood before them and said, "Peace!" With love and great happiness at seeing him again, they fell at his feet. Even though Jesus had promised to come back from the dead, they had not completely believed it would happen. Now it had!

God asks us to believe some things that may be hard to understand. Jesus is the Son of God. He can only tell us what is true. And so we believe and trust everything that Jesus tells us about God his Father. Our belief is called *faith*. We pray that God will always give us a greater and stronger faith.

By dying and rising from the dead, Jesus overcame sin. He made it possible for us to live forever with God in heaven. He fulfilled God's promise to send a Savior who would give us everlasting life.

On Easter we celebrate and we sing, "Alleluia!" which means, "Praise the Lord!" We promise to be good followers of Jesus by renewing our baptismal promises, which were made for us by our parents and godparents when we were baptized.

On Easter the church is decorated with white, the color of victory, purity and joy. The priest wears a white chasuble and the altar is covered with a white cloth. A white cloth might also hang on the cross to show that Jesus has left the tomb. Many times, the altar is surrounded by lilies. Lilies stand for goodness and beauty and they remind us of our new life. We joyfully sing praises to our risen Lord: "Jesus Christ is risen today, Alleluia!"

The season of Easter lasts fifty days. We can be "Easter People" by showing our joy to all, by treating others with love and kindness, and especially by sharing the message about the new life Jesus has given us.

 **Let's Pray!**

Alleluia! You have risen from the dead, Lord Jesus! You have won new life for us! We praise and thank you for your life, for your words, and for your death and resurrection. Help us to follow you, Jesus, so that one day we'll live with you forever in the joy of heaven. Amen.

Let's Do a Project!

1

Create an anagram poster. Using the letters from the words ALLELUIA! HE IS RISEN!, make other words that show your faith and how you will share the good news of Jesus' resurrection.

Here are some words you can make:

Resurrection	Cross
Lord	Caring
Share	Kindness
Miracle	Praise Him!
Life	Heaven
Love	Eternal Life
Jesus	And many others…

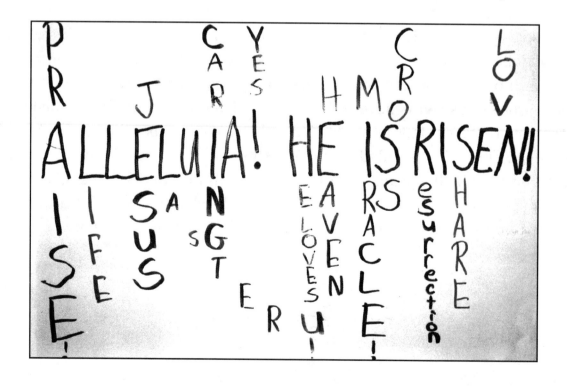

Use large yellow letters for ALLE-LUIA! HE IS RISEN! and smaller letters of other bright colors to fill in the other words. Hang your poster in your home or classroom.

2

Share messages of new life with the residents of a nearby nursing home, or with elderly neighbors. Draw a colorful Easter or springtime picture on pieces of white paper. Write a cheery message of new life on them. Roll up the pictures and place a small rubber band around them to keep them rolled up.

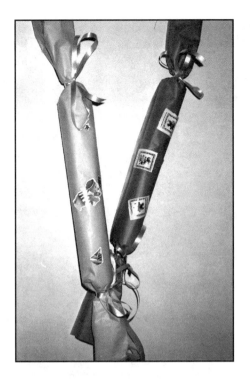

Then wrap colored tissue paper around them and tie the ends closed with colorful ribbons. Decorate them with colorful stickers.

With your parents or an older brother or sister, visit the nursing home or your neighbors' homes to deliver the new life messages.

3

Celebrate Jesus' passion, death and resurrection by making a Holy Week mobile. Draw the symbols listed below on pieces of thin white cardboard.

Cut them out according to their shapes. On the back of each picture, print the name of the day it stands for, for example, EASTER SUNDAY. Color in the pictures and then punch a hole at the top of each shape. Cut pieces of string that are 6 to 12 inches long. Tie one end to the top of each picture.

Use a coat hanger to make the frame for the mobile. Wrap the hanger with ribbon, brightly colored crepe paper streamers or strips of tissue paper. Tie the pictures to the frame to create the hanging parts of your mobile.

Cut a rectangle about 1 in x 6 in and write HOLY WEEK on it. Attach it to the frame of the mobile.

Symbols to Use for the Mobile Pictures:

Palm Sunday—palm branches, donkey, a robe and crown

Holy Thursday—wine goblet, grapes, flat pieces of bread, water jar and towel

Good Friday—cross, crown of thorns, lightning, hammer and nail

Holy Saturday—large grave, stone

Easter Sunday—angel, risen Jesus, burial cloths, Easter lilies, cross draped with burial cloth

4

Easter baskets and Easter candy symbolize the overflowing kindness of Jesus in rising from the dead to rescue us from sin. Instead of keeping your basket and candy only for yourself, why not keep it near the front door where you can share it with your friends and family members? That would be a kind, generous deed that would please Jesus very much!

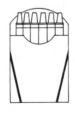

Turn to page 121 for a picture to color!

Ascension Day

Forty days after Easter, or in some western dioceses, the following Sunday

After Jesus rose from the dead on Easter Sunday, he stayed on earth for forty days. He still had things to do and people to see.

On each of the five Sundays after Easter, we hear Gospel readings about how Jesus visited his friends and taught them more lessons.

Jesus had so much to share with his followers that each moment was precious. We all know how hard it is to say goodbye and to leave behind someone we love. Jesus felt the same way.

When Jesus visited his disciples, they were able to see with their own eyes that he was alive. Jesus let them touch the wounds in his hands, feet and side. He wanted them to be able to believe with all their hearts that he really had died on the cross and risen from the dead. They did believe and were filled with wonder, joy and gratitude.

Then Jesus gave the disciples a very important mission or assignment. "Go to everyone around the world and tell them about me," he said. "Teach them the lessons I gave you. Baptize them in the name of the Father, and of the Son, and of the Holy Spirit. Everyone who believes in me will be saved and will live with me forever in heaven."

The disciples were happy to do this mission for Jesus. We are disciples of Jesus too. We can go out and share what we know about Jesus with others. We can spread the good news about Jesus by what we say and what we do.

Finally, it was the end of Jesus' time on earth. Jesus was with some of his friends when suddenly he was lifted up before their eyes in a cloud. They could no longer see him. Then two angels appeared and told them that just as Jesus had been taken up to heaven, he would come back again one day. That made the disciples happy.

We call Jesus' going up to heaven the *ascension*. We go to Mass on Ascension Day to celebrate Jesus' going home to heaven. Just as we love to go home to our families and friends after being away, Jesus was thrilled to return to God his Father. He had finished the special work that his Father had given him to do, and God welcomed him home with joy and love. We know that God the Father, Jesus, and his Holy Spirit are waiting for us to join them in heaven at the end of our time on earth. This thought makes us happy!

On Ascension Day, we remember that Jesus has also given us the job of spreading his word to all people. We are his messengers, just like the first disciples. We can share Jesus' message of love by speaking about him to our friends, family and people we meet. Just as important as words, our kind and good actions let everyone know that Jesus is alive in us.

Let's Pray!

Jesus, on the Feast of the Ascension we celebrate the day you returned to heaven. For forty days after your resurrection, you shared with and taught your disciples. Then your mission on earth was finished. It was time to go back to heaven. Help us to live the way you've taught us to, Jesus. This is how we can spread the good news of your Gospel everywhere we go. Amen.

Let's Do a Project!

1

With your class or family, hold a party to celebrate Jesus' return to heaven.

A week or two before Ascension, make invitations or signs inviting others to join you for this special occasion. On the invitation, ask each guest to come ready to share his or her favorite memory of Jesus—a story from one of the gospels or a saying or teaching of Jesus.

Make a cake for the party and write on it: "Jesus, you are always with us!" Decorate the room with banners that say things like "Thank you, Lord!" "We believe that you will come again, Jesus!" and "Help us to spread your Gospel everywhere."

At the party, celebrate together by sharing your memories and thanking Jesus for coming to earth to win eternal life for us.

2

If you have Internet access, copy out a story of something Jesus said or did from one of the gospels. E-mail it to a friend or relative with the message: "I thought I'd send you some Good News today." If you don't have e-mail, write or type out the story and send it by regular mail.

3

Draw a picture of Mary and the Apostles looking up at the sky as Jesus goes up to heaven through the clouds. Glue on cotton to cover the sky with clouds. At the bottom of the picture, write: "Jesus, I love you!"

Turn to page 123 for a picture to color!

Pentecost

The Sunday that comes seven weeks, or about fifty days, after Easter

After Jesus ascended to heaven, his Apostles and Mary his mother stayed together and prayed. The Apostles remembered that Jesus had given them the mission of spreading his message to everyone in the world. But they didn't feel ready to preach yet. Before returning to heaven, Jesus had promised that the Holy Spirit would come to them to give them power. They didn't have long to wait.

On the Jewish Feast of Pentecost, Mary and the Apostles were praying together. Suddenly, they heard a loud noise that sounded like wind blowing through the house. As they looked around, they saw little flames of fire above each of their heads. They were all filled with the Holy Spirit. Then they understood God's plan better. God wanted them to live together as a community of believers who would try to do his will on earth. (We call this community the Church.)

The Holy Spirit made the Apostles strong and filled them with God's gifts. He helped them to understand who Jesus is—the Son of God who came to earth to teach us about God the Father, and to bring us one day to heaven. The Holy Spirit makes us strong and fills us with God's gifts too!

On Pentecost the Jewish people who were gathered in Jerusalem from many different countries were amazed to hear the Apostles speaking in each of their own languages. This was another gift of the Holy Spirit.

God gave us Jesus to save us and to teach us. Then God gave us the Holy Spirit to fill us with his gifts. These gifts help us to live the way Jesus has asked us to. They help us to teach others about Jesus.

Each of us receives gifts from the Holy Spirit. On Pentecost Sunday let's thank the Holy Spirit for his gifts. Let's use them to be messengers of Jesus in the world!

Let's Pray!

Holy Spirit, on Pentecost you came down on Mary and the Apostles to fill them with your gifts. You come to us, too. You fill us with all the gifts we need to live as Jesus teaches us. Some of these gifts are understanding, courage and love. Thank you, Holy Spirit! Help us to use your gifts well! Amen.

Let's Do a Project!

1

When the Holy Spirit came to the Apostles on Pentecost, one of the gifts he gave them was the ability to speak that day in a language that all the people understood. This was a sign that God wanted the message of Jesus to be told to people of every country on earth. Draw a picture of the world in the middle of a sheet of paper or posterboard. All around the world, write the words "God," "Jesus" and "Holy Spirit" in as many languages as you can. Use yellow for the words meaning "God," green for "Jesus" and red for "Holy Spirit."

Work with your teacher or family members to find the words in foreign language dictionaries or books, or use this list:

(English)	God	Jesus	Holy Spirit
(French)	Dieu	Jesu	le Saint Esprit
(Spanish)	Dios	Jesús	el Espíritu Santo
(German)	Gött	Jesus	Heiliger Geist
(Vietnamese)	Thiên Chua	Giêsu	Chua Thanh Linh

2

Pray the third glorious mystery of the rosary in which we remember the coming of the Holy Spirit on Pentecost. Ask Mary, who prayed with the Apostles as they prepared for that first Pentecost, to help you to become a better follower of Jesus. Mary is the mother of all the friends and messengers of Jesus. She'll be sure to help you and to show you how to spread Jesus' Good News to your friends.

3

Make a Pentecost windsock. It will be a reminder of how the Holy Spirit blows and moves in us. A symbol of the Holy Spirit is the dove.

Draw a 9-inch-long dove shape on a sheet of firm white paper to make the body of the windsock. Color the edges of the dove red. (This is the color usually used for the Holy Spirit.) Bend the wings of the dove toward each other and staple them together.

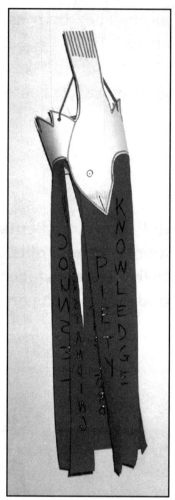

Then cut seven 20-inch-long pieces of red streamers. Use a black marker to write one of the gifts of the Holy Spirit on each streamer. Here is a list of the gifts of the Holy Spirit:

Wisdom
Knowledge
Understanding
Piety (Love)
Counsel
Fortitude (Courage)
Fear of the Lord

Glue the streamers to the tail of the dove. Punch three holes at the head of the dove. Tie red yarn through the holes to make a loop for hanging the windsock. Hang your windsock outside in good weather.

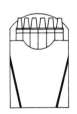

Turn to page 125 for a picture to color!

Ordinary Time and Other Feasts

We call any days that are not Advent, Christmas, Lent, or Easter, *Ordinary Time*. The Sundays in Ordinary Time are all numbered. For example, we say "The Tenth Sunday in Ordinary Time," or "the Thirtieth Sunday in Ordinary Time." During Ordinary Time, we try to pay attention to the lessons God gives us for everyday life.

Green is the color of Ordinary Time. The chasuble worn by the priest at Mass is green. The cloth covering the altar may be green, too. In our Church, the color green stands for hope, growth and life. As we learn the lessons God teaches us in each Mass, we grow in our hope to live with God and one another one day in heaven.

There are also many feast days during Ordinary Time. Some of the main ones are Trinity Sunday, the Feast of Corpus Christi, the Feast of the Sacred Heart of Jesus, the Feast of the Transfiguration, and the Feast of Christ the King. During Ordinary Time we also celebrate some special days in honor of the saints. Two of these are the Birth of John the Baptist and the Feast of Saints Peter and Paul.

65

Feast of the Holy Trinity

Trinity Sunday
The Sunday after Pentecost

On this feast we remember a great *mystery*. In our Church, a mystery is something that we know is true, but that we can't understand. The mystery we celebrate today is that there is only one God in three divine Persons. These divine Persons are the almighty Father, his only Son, and the Holy Spirit. We call God the Father, God the Son and God the Holy Spirit the *Holy Trinity.*

God the Father created everything. God the Son came to save us from sin. God the Holy Spirit makes us holy by his action in our lives. We adore our one God in three Persons. We make an act of faith in the Holy Trinity each time we make the sign of the cross and say, "In the name of the Father, and of the Son, and of the Holy Spirit. Amen."

The three Persons of the Holy Trinity came to live in us when we were baptized. Through God's great love for us, we share in the life of the Holy Trinity!

 **Let's Pray!**

Glory to the Father, and to the Son, and to the Holy Spirit: as it was in the beginning, is now, and will be forever. Amen.

Let's Do a Project!

1

Ask your parents or teacher to show you how to make the sign of the cross. Bless yourself with the sign of the cross whenever you feel you need God's special help or protection.

2

Draw a three-leaf clover. On each leaf, write the names of one of the Persons of the Holy Trinity, the Father, Son, and Holy Spirit. Underneath your picture write: "There are three Persons in one God. This is the Holy Trinity." Hang this poster in your room.

Turn to page 127 for a picture to color!

Feast of the Body and Blood of Christ

Corpus Christi
In the United States, the Sunday after Trinity Sunday

The Church sets aside a day each year to give special thanks for the *Holy Eucharist*. The Holy Eucharist is the true Body and Blood of Jesus Christ. The Latin name for this day is "Corpus Christi." This means the "Body of Christ."

On the Feast of Corpus Christi we hear the story of the Last Supper, when Jesus changed bread into his Body and wine into his Blood. We may also have a *procession* in honor of the Holy Eucharist at our parish church. A procession is a special kind of parade in which we honor God, Mary, or the saints by praying or singing together as we walk from one place to another.

Jesus gave his Body and Blood to the Apostles at the Last Supper. At Mass, he also gives us this special food. We receive Jesus' Body and Blood in Holy Communion. This special food gives us the strength to live and act as God wants us to.

After Mass, the Holy Eucharist is kept in the *tabernacle*, a beautiful, special box-like shrine in our Church. Jesus is really and truly present in the Holy Eucharist, even though we can't see him with our eyes. He waits for us to visit him there. We *adore* Jesus present in the Holy Eucharist. This means that we worship and honor him. The Feast of the Body and Blood of Christ reminds us of how lucky we are to have Jesus so near us!

Let's Pray!

Jesus, I adore you present in all tabernacles all over the world. Thank you for the wonderful gift of the Holy Eucharist! Even though I can't see you, I know and believe that you are present in this sacrament. You watch over me and listen to my prayers. You are my very best friend, Jesus. Amen.

Let's Do a Project!

1

Ask your parents or teachers to show you how to genuflect whenever you enter or leave your church, where Jesus is present in the Holy Eucharist. A genuflection is a special way of honoring Jesus.

2

Make a visit to Jesus in the Holy Eucharist. Talk to him about everything that's in your heart. Thank Jesus for his love. Tell him things that you are happy or sad about. Ask him to help poor and sick people and all those who are suffering in any way. Be sure to remember not to talk out loud when you're in church, out of respect for Jesus.

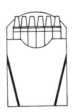

Turn to page 129 for a picture to color!

Feast of the Sacred Heart of Jesus

BEHOLD THE HEART...

The Friday following the second Sunday after Pentecost

We call Jesus' heart *sacred* because this word means *holy* or *belonging to God*. On the Feast of the Sacred Heart, we thank Jesus for his love for us. The heart of Jesus is a sign of his great love.

When you place your hand over your heart, you can feel it pumping the blood through your body. This keeps you alive. Your heart is the center of your life and your feelings.

In the same way, Jesus is the center of our lives as Christians. The heart is a symbol of Jesus because it is his love that keeps our souls alive. Jesus' love helps us to live lives filled with goodness.

Sometimes the Sacred Heart symbol is shown surrounded by fire. This means that Jesus' love is like a fire that catches and spreads quickly among his people. The heart and the fire remind us that we are to love others and spread Jesus' love to everyone we meet.

Going to Mass and receiving Holy Communion on the first Friday of every month, or making a holy hour of prayer in honor of Jesus' Sacred Heart are ways to show our love for Jesus and to ask pardon for those people who don't accept his love.

Let's Pray!

70

Jesus, your Sacred Heart is a sign to all of the love you have for us. Help us to love one another as you love us. Let your love overcome all the hatred and violence in our world. Make our hearts like yours, Jesus. We want to spread your peace and joy everywhere. Amen.

Let's Do a Project!

1

The heart is a popular symbol of love. It's used especially for Valentine's Day, when heart-shaped cards are exchanged. Celebrate the Feast of the Sacred Heart by making and giving Valentine-like cards to your family and friends. On the front of the cards, make a picture of Jesus' Sacred Heart with the flames of his love. On the inside, write messages like: "Happy Feast of the Sacred Heart! Remember, Jesus loves you!"

2

Make a Sacred Heart collage. From old magazines and newspapers, cut out pictures of people's faces: old, young, rich, poor and of every color and background. Put as many as you can fit on a 20 in x 24 in posterboard. In the center, glue a picture of the Sacred Heart of Jesus, with the words, "Come to me, all you who labor…" (Mt 11:28).

3

Make a Sacred Heart badge for your backpack. Cut a heart shape out of a plastic lid. Cover it with red foil or cellophane. Cut a cross shape out of white cardboard. Color or paint it gold or silver and glue it to the center of the heart. Now turn the heart over and tape a large safety pin to it. Pin the badge to your backpack to remind people that God loves them!

Turn to page 131 for a picture to color!

Feast of the Birth of Saint John the Baptist

June 24

Before Jesus began teaching, another special man went out among the people to tell them to get ready for Jesus. He was a relative of Jesus, the son of Mary's cousin Elizabeth. His name was John, and he was called "The Baptist." This is his story.

Elizabeth was married to Zechariah. They were both good and holy people. But they were very old and sad that they had never had children.

One day in the temple, an angel appeared to Zechariah. The angel told him that he and his wife would have a son named John who would help people turn to God. Zechariah was surprised. He didn't believe the angel. Because of this, the angel told him that he wouldn't be able to speak another word until it all came true.

So Zechariah couldn't speak until the baby was born. When Elizabeth and Zechariah named their son John, Zechariah was able to talk again and he began praising God. Soon people came to know that John was holy.

When John grew up, he lived in the desert. He wore simple clothes made of camel hair and a rough belt of leather. He ate locusts, insects of the desert, and wild honey. He reminded the people of another prophet of long ago called Elijah.

John the Baptist asked people to stop sinning. He asked them to get ready for the coming of their Savior. To show that their hearts and lives were clean and ready for Jesus, John poured water over them in the Jordan River. This was a kind of baptism.

Some people thought that John was the promised savior. But John told them that he wasn't. He explained that he was only preparing the way for someone much greater than himself.

On this feast, we celebrate the birth of Saint John the Baptist. We thank him for the example he gives us. We, too, can help others not to sin, by sharing our love and knowledge of Jesus.

Let's Pray!

Dear God, you sent John the Baptist to prepare the people for the coming of your Son Jesus. Help us to be like John. Help us every day to make more room for Jesus in our lives and in our world. Amen.

Let's Do a Project!

1

On a large piece of white posterboard, make a picture of John baptizing Jesus. Draw John in his rough clothes. Remember the dove over the head of Jesus as John pours water over him. At the bottom of the picture write: "Thank you, John the Baptist, for baptizing our Lord!"

2

Saint John the Baptist dared to be different. Get together with your friends or brothers and sisters and write your own words to the tune of a song you already know and like. The words should be about the courage that it takes to be more like Jesus, even if it means being different and *not doing what everyone else is doing.*

3

Saint John the Baptist is a patron saint of *conversion* or turning away from sin. Do some detective work. Bring home your parish bulletin and look up the day and hour when the sacrament of

Penance is celebrated at your church. Decide on a time you can go to confession in order to turn away from sin and grow closer to Jesus. Mark the date on your calendar so you won't forget!

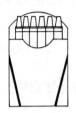

Turn to page 133 for a picture to color!

Feast of Saints Peter and Paul

June 29

Saints Peter and Paul were both important followers of Jesus, and we can learn a lot from their lives.

Peter was one of Jesus' first twelve *Apostles*. (An apostle is a messenger, or someone who is sent.) Peter's name had been "Simon," but Jesus gave him the new name "Peter," which means "rock." Peter was the rock on which Jesus would build his Church.

Peter was very close to Jesus and loved him very much. But sometimes his faith was weak. Once, in the middle of a storm, Jesus began walking on the water toward a boat carrying his frightened apostles. They grew even more afraid when they saw Jesus walking on the water. Peter called out, "If it's really you, Jesus, let *me* walk on the water too!"

Jesus told Peter to get out of the boat and walk on the water. Peter obeyed. But he became afraid as he saw the wind and waves, and he started to sink. "Lord, save me!" Peter cried. And Jesus did.

Another time, near the end of Jesus' life, Jesus said that Peter would soon tell others that he didn't know Jesus. Peter answered that that would never happen. But later, when Jesus had been arrested, Peter said three times that he didn't know Jesus. When he realized what he had done, and that Jesus' words had been true, Peter cried in sorrow.

Even though Peter's faith was sometimes weak, Jesus knew that his love and strength were great. So Jesus asked him to be the leader of his people. Peter became the first Bishop of Rome. Today the Bishop of Rome is the successor of Saint Peter. We call him the *Pope*, which means *Father*.

After Jesus' death, Peter spread the word about Jesus. He was able to perform miracles to show Jesus' power. He had an important dream that taught him that God's love and Jesus' teachings were meant for all people in the world. In the end, Peter died for Jesus in Rome. This means he was a *martyr*.

Paul, instead, didn't know Jesus when Jesus was living on earth. As a young man, Paul was called Saul. He didn't believe in Jesus. In fact, he hated the followers of Jesus and even tried to kill them. But one day, he saw a bright light and heard the voice of Jesus.

From that time, his name was changed to Paul. He also had a change of heart and became one of Jesus' greatest apostles.

Saint Paul was the Church's first great missionary. He traveled thousands of miles to tell as many people as he could about Jesus. After he met people in his travels, he wrote them many letters to continue teaching them and to support them in their new lives as Christians. Paul also died for Jesus in Rome. He was also a martyr.

The part of the New Testament called the Acts of the Apostles tells the stories of Peter and Paul after Jesus' death. The first half is mostly about Peter and the second half is about Paul. Peter and Paul are wonderful examples of how people can be changed and made strong by the love of God and faith in Jesus.

We can pray to grow stronger in our faith so that like Saints Peter and Paul, we too can be missionaries and spread God's message to everyone we meet.

 ## Let's Pray!

Dear Jesus, how we wish we could have known you while you were here on earth! But thanks to your Apostles, Peter and Paul, we know about your life and your love. Thank you, Jesus, for making them leaders in your Church. And thank you Saints Peter and Paul for spreading Jesus' word all over the world. Make our faith as strong as a rock, Saint Peter. Help us to be mes-

sengers of the Gospel, Saint Paul. We want to build up the Church as you did. Amen.

Let's Do a Project!

1

Peter was a fisherman by trade. But when Jesus called Peter to follow him, he promised that from then on Peter would fish for people, not for fish.

When Peter went fishing, he used wide nets that would catch many fish at once, instead of a fishing pole that would catch only one at a time. Make your own net to hang in your room. It will remind you that you too can be a "fisher of people" by telling others about Jesus.

Here's how to make your net. (**Hint:** You might want to ask a grownup to help you with this project.) Work with a partner. Cut eighteen pieces of 18-inch rough brown string. (Newspaper tying twine is perfect.) One partner will hold the strings tight as the net is being formed. The other partner will tie the strings. Take turns doing both jobs.

Partner A begins by holding the ends of one string and pulling it into a tight line in front of himself or herself.

This is the first horizontal string, or a string that goes sideways. Partner A then folds the string in half to find the middle. Now Partner B ties a string to the middle of Partner A's string. Next Partner B ties four more strings to the left and four more strings to the right. The strings should be about 1½ inches apart from each other. Each string should be attached with a tight double or square knot. These are the vertical strings, or strings that go up and down.

Partner A continues to hold the first string pulled tightly like a frame. Partner B then begins to tie the second horizontal string to the nine vertical strings. Partner B starts by tying the new string to the vertical string on the far right, making a knot about 1½ inches down from the first horizontal string. Partner B continues tying this new string to all the vertical strings, moving from right to left in a straight line.

Now Partner B takes a turn holding the net, grasping the two ends of the second horizontal string. Partner A ties a third horizontal string to the vertical strings in the same way described above. Continue taking turns holding the net and tying the strings until all nine horizontal strings are tied to the nine vertical strings. When all the strings have been tied, you'll have your own net!

2

Peter was sometimes weak in his faith, but Jesus brought out the best in him. Jesus did this by loving him and giving him an important role in his new Church. Jesus also forgave Peter for the times his faith wasn't strong.

Think of ways that *you* are sometimes weak. Then think of wrong things you sometimes do. Write them down on a piece of paper. Next think about how Jesus helps you to change. Write a prayer asking Jesus to help you change for the better, just as he helped Peter.

3

Pretend that you are a missionary like Paul and that you have told people far away about Jesus. Write a letter, just like Paul did, to the new followers of Jesus.

Choose one of Jesus' teachings—a parable, lesson or event from his life—and write about it to the new Christians. Tell them how they can use this message in their lives. Write words to encourage them to grow in their faith.

Send your letter to a friend or family member to share the Good News of Jesus.

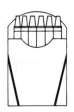

Turn to page 135 for a picture to color!

Feast of the Transfiguration

August 6

On this feast we remember the day Jesus took three of his friends and apostles, Peter, James and John, to a high mountain. Suddenly, they saw him change or become *transfigured*. His face was shining as brightly as the sun. His clothes became dazzlingly white. The three apostles saw Jesus talking to Moses and Elijah, two Old Testament prophets. When a cloud covered Jesus, God the Father's voice spoke from heaven. He said, "This is my beloved Son who makes me very happy. Listen to him!"

It's easy to imagine how Jesus' friends felt at seeing this wonderful sight and hearing God's voice! At the transfiguration Jesus showed his closest apostles his divine glory. This helped to prepare them to see Jesus suffer and die for us.

 ## Let's Pray!

Lord Jesus, we want to listen to you, as God the Father said at the transfiguration. We believe that you are God. Make our faith grow more and more each day. Amen.

Let's Do a Project!

1

Read the story of Jesus' transfiguration in the Bible. You'll find it in Lk 9:28–36. Next think quietly about this story. What do you think it means to "listen to Jesus"? Write down some of the ways that you can put what Jesus tells you into practice (for example, loving other people as he loves you, forgiving others, etc.).

2

Make your own comic strip to tell the story of the transfiguration. Draw each of the main scenes and print the parts of the story below them. Share your comic strip with your family and friends.

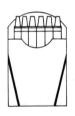

Turn to page 137 for a picture to color!

Feast of Mary's Assumption into Heaven

August 15

Mary, the mother of Jesus, led a very good and holy life. She always obeyed God and never sinned. She is the best example we have of a person who lived her life for God.

God gave Mary a wonderful gift at the end of her life on earth. Because she is the sinless mother of his Son, God brought Mary's body and soul to heaven. God's taking of Mary into heaven is called the *assumption*.

On this feast day, we honor Mary and remember how God honored her by taking her to heaven in this special way. How happy she was to be with Jesus again in heaven! How happy we will all be with God and with the people we love one day in heaven!

 **Let's Pray!**

Mary, you had the special honor of being taken body and soul to heaven because you are the Mother of God. From heaven, you watch over us. Pray for us to Jesus. We want to join you in heaven one day. We want to live there with God and with all the saints forever. Amen.

Let's Do a Project!

1

Draw a picture of Mary on a bright blue sky. Fill the sky with pieces of cotton to make the clouds. Hang this picture on your refrigerator door in time for August 15.

2

Pray the fourth glorious mystery of the rosary, the assumption, for all those who are preparing to go to heaven, especially those who are very sick or elderly and have no one to pray for them.

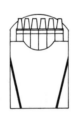

Turn to page 139 for a picture to color!

Feast of the Birth of Mary

September 8

On this day we celebrate Mary's birthday. This is a special birthday because Mary is a special person. God chose her to be the mother of his Son, Jesus. A very old tradition in the Church tells us that Mary's parents were Saint Ann and Saint Joachim.

Mary is the most important saint of our Church. She is honored on several different feast days. Some of these are the Immaculate Conception, Mary the Mother of God, the Annunciation, and the Assumption.

When Mary was born, God gave the world a great gift. He already knew that she would be the mother of his Son. This is why Mary was born free of any sin and why she never sinned during her whole life.

Mary, a simple human being just like us, has shown us how to have strong faith in God. She also teaches us how to obey God's will.

By honoring the birth and life of Mary, and by trying to be like her, we can come closer to God the Father and to Jesus, the Son of God and son of Mary.

 **Let's Pray!**

Happy Birthday, Mary! How wonderful you are! We thank God for making you the mother of his Son, and the mother of all of us, too! Amen.

Let's Do a Project!

1

Have a birthday party for Mary! Decorate the room with banners that say "Happy Birthday, Mary!" Bake a cake and decorate it with a crown, a symbol for Mary, the Queen of Heaven. Give everyone a birthday candle and gather around the cake. Ask each person to say something special about Mary and her life. Then have that person put his or her candle on the cake and light it.

When all the candles are on the cake, join hands and offer a prayer or song to Mary. Sing "Happy Birthday" to Mary as you blow out the candles.

2

Ask your parents or teacher to rent you a video about the Blessed Mother. You might want to see one about the times Mary appeared to Saint Bernadette at Lourdes, or the times she visited Lucia, Jacinta and Francisco at Fatima. (You can also rent animated stories of Lourdes and Fatima from any of the addresses at the back of this book.)

Ask your parents, brothers, sisters or friends to watch the video with you. After watching it, talk about your favorite part of the video and explain why you liked it.

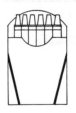

Turn to page 141 for a picture to color!

All Saints' Day

November 1

As we grow up, it's good to have heroes and heroines to admire. The best kind of hero or heroine is the one who makes the world a better place for others. Learning about such persons helps us to try harder to do well, so that we can be like them.

There are many Christian heroes and heroines who have lived before us. They are called the *saints.* The saints are friends of God, and they can help us to come closer to God too. By *canonizing* them or officially naming them saints, the Church honors these holy people in a special way and helps us to learn from their good example.

When we learn about the saints, we find out that they were ordinary people just like us. But all of them had great faith in God. This strong faith helped them to do wonderful things in their lives. Most of the saints are known for helping others, especially the poor and the sick.

Everyone who is in heaven living in the presence of God is also called a saint, even though the Church may never officially name them one.

On the Feast of All Saints we honor all of these holy friends of God. We go to Mass to thank God for giving us the saints. We listen to the gospel story of the Beatitudes, the lesson Jesus gave us about how to be holy and happy. We pray that we will live good and holy lives so that when it's our turn to die, God will welcome us to heaven to live with him and with all of the saints forever and ever!

 **Let's Pray!**

Heavenly Father, you bless us each with gifts and talents. We pray that like the saints, we will use our gifts and talents to bring your love to the whole world. Lord, may the saints and their stories show us how to follow Jesus more closely. Please help us to become saints too! Amen.

Let's Do a Project!

1

Choose a saint that is special to you. It may be your own patron saint (the saint you're named after) or one whose story you've found in a book of lives of the saints. After reading his or her story, make a list of some of the good and loving things this saint did. Then make a list of some of the good and loving things you can do to imitate this saint.

Draw a poster showing your saint standing next to you. Under the saint's picture, copy the list of his or her good deeds. Under your picture, copy the list of the good deeds you want to try to do. Hang the poster on your closet door.

2

Ask your parents to get you a book that tells the stories of many of the saints. (You can obtain one from any of the addresses listed at the back of this book.) Or check one out of the library. Read these stories often and think about them.

3

Pick a favorite saint. Try to find more information on him or her. You might even be able to find a holy card, medal, or statue of your favorite saint. Tell a Web friend about your special "friend in heaven."

Turn to page 143 for a picture to color!

All Souls' Day

November 2

On the day after All Saints' Day, we celebrate All Souls' Day. On this feast we remember everyone who has ever lived and died. We pray for our family members and friends and for our ancestors. We also pray for those people whom we don't know. We ask God to give all those who have died happiness and peace in their new life with him.

One day our life on earth will come to an end. But Jesus has taught us that our life will never end. It will only change when we die. It makes us happy to think about this on All Souls' Day. We know and believe that one day we will be together with God and with our family and friends again in our new life.

 ## Let's Pray!

Dear God, today we think of all the people who have died. We remember them, and we pray for them in a special way. We pray for our family members and friends who have died. (Say their names here.) We also pray for those people whom we don't know. God, please give them all a new life filled with love and light and happiness—a life with you that will never end! Amen.

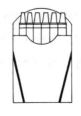

Let's Do a Project!

1

Make an "All Souls' Day" banner. Using a wide sheet of light blue paper or posterboard, create a sky or "heaven" background. Cut a yellow sun with rays from yellow paper and a crescent moon from gold paper. Cut out fluffy white cloud shapes. On each cloud, write the name of a family member or friend who has died. (Ask your parents to help you remember and write down the names.) Glue the cloud shapes onto the sky background.

2

On All Souls' Day, place your banner in a spot where the whole family can see it. Get together before your family meal to remember those whose names are on the banner. Say a prayer for them, asking God to let you all be together again in heaven one day.

During your meal, talk about the wonderful times you shared with your relatives and friends who have died. Honor their lives by remembering the good things they did for you and for others. Talk about the ways in which they made the world a better place.

3

Go to visit a cemetery. If you have no family members or friends buried there, pray for the people who are buried there—old and young, rich and poor.

Turn to page 145 for a picture to color!

Feast of Christ the King

The last Sunday of November

On the last Sunday of the Church's year, we celebrate the Feast of Christ the King. Jesus is King of all because he has conquered sin and death. He came to lead us into his kingdom, the kingdom of God.

Jesus is not like the ordinary kings we've heard of. He doesn't rule over just one country or kingdom. He rules over every person, every family, every nation and the whole universe. Jesus rules over all of us with love, and his kingdom will last forever!

 **Let's Pray!**

Jesus, King of our hearts and our lives, help us to obey you always. You know what is best for us. You want what is best for us. We believe in your love! Amen.

Let's Do a Project!

1

Search old newspapers and magazines for pictures of presidents, prime ministers, governors or senators. Cut out as many as you can find, and paste or tape them to a large white posterboard. At the top of the poster draw a picture of Jesus. Under the picture, print the words: Jesus is the greatest Ruler of all the world!

2

Draw a crown on a piece of cardboard. Cut it out and cover it with aluminum foil or gold wrapping paper. Glue different beads, sequins, glitter or imitation "jewels" on it. Lay your crown at the foot of a crucifix in your home, or have your parents place it above a crucifix in time for the Feast of Christ the King.

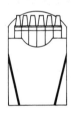

Turn to page 147 for a picture to color!

We have completed our year with God. The cycle will soon start over with a new season of Advent. Then it will be time to go back to the beginning of this book and review the meaning of our different holy days and seasons again. Although we are a year older, we can all continue to learn as we grow in age, knowledge, and wisdom.

Every year can be wonderful, if we spend it with God!

Listing of Holy Days of Obligation

Unless otherwise designated by the bishop of a diocese, the holy days of obligation in the United States are:

Mary, Mother of God—January 1 (except when it falls on a Saturday or Monday)

Ascension of Our Lord—forty days after Easter, or in some western dioceses, the following Sunday

Assumption of the Blessed Virgin Mary—August 15 (except when it falls on a Saturday or Monday)

All Saints' Day—November 1 (except when it falls on a Saturday or Monday)

Mary's Immaculate Conception—December 8

Christmas—December 25

Unless otherwise designated, the holy days of obligation in Canada are:

Mary, Mother of God—January 1

Christmas—December 25

Our Year with God

Reproducible Coloring Pages

of Catholic Holy Days and Feasts

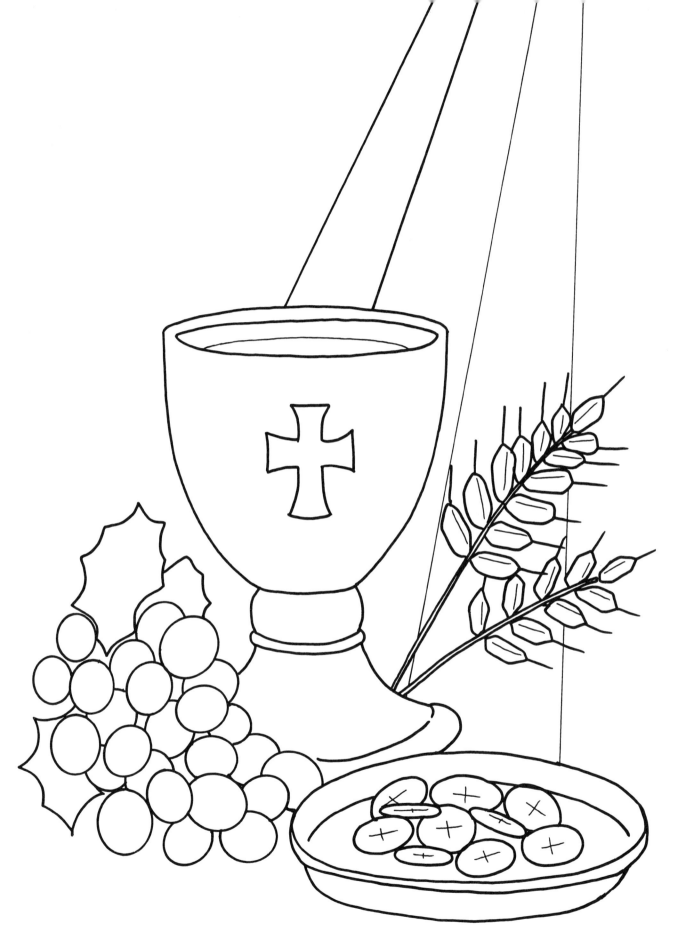

Pauline
BOOKS & MEDIA

The Daughters of St. Paul operate book and media centers at the following addresses. Visit, call or write the one nearest you today, or find us on the World Wide Web, www.pauline.org.

CALIFORNIA
3908 Sepulveda Blvd., Culver City, CA 90230;
  310-397-8676
5945 Balboa Ave., San Diego, CA 92111;
  858-565-9181
46 Geary Street, San Francisco, CA 94108;
  415-781-5180

FLORIDA
145 S.W. 107th Ave., Miami, FL 33174;
  305-559-6715

HAWAII
1143 Bishop Street, Honolulu, HI 96813;
  808-521-2731
Neighbor Islands call: 800-259-8463

ILLINOIS
172 North Michigan Ave., Chicago, IL 60601;
  312-346-4228

LOUISIANA
4403 Veterans Memorial Blvd., Metairie, LA 70006;
  504-887-7631

MASSACHUSETTS
Rte. 1, 885 Providence Hwy., Dedham, MA 02026;
  781-326-5385

MISSOURI
9804 Watson Rd., St. Louis, MO 63126;
  314-965-3512

NEW JERSEY
561 U.S. Route 1, Wick Plaza, Edison, NJ 08817;
  732-572-1200

NEW YORK
150 East 52nd Street, New York, NY 10022;
  212-754-1110
78 Fort Place, Staten Island, NY 10301;
  718-447-5071

OHIO
2105 Ontario Street (at Prospect Ave.), Cleveland,
  OH 44115; 216-621-9427

PENNSYLVANIA
9171-A Roosevelt Blvd., Philadelphia, PA 19114;
215-676-9494

SOUTH CAROLINA
243 King Street, Charleston, SC 29401;
  843-577-0175

TENNESSEE
4811 Poplar Ave., Memphis, TN 38117;
  901-761-2987

TEXAS
114 Main Plaza, San Antonio, TX 78205;
  210-224-8101

VIRGINIA
1025 King Street, Alexandria, VA 22314;
  703-549-3806

CANADA
3022 Dufferin Street, Toronto, Ontario, Canada
  M6B 3T5; 416-781-9131
1155 Yonge Street, Toronto, Ontario, Canada
  M4T 1W2; 416-934-3440

¡También somos su fuente para libros, videos y música en Español!